UNIVERSITY OF CAMBRIDGE
RESEARCH CENTRE FOR INTERNATIONAL LAW

HERSCH LAUTERPACHT MEMORIAL LECTURES

COMPETITION POLICY AND MERGER CONTROL IN THE SINGLE EUROPEAN MARKET

by

THE RT. HON. SIR LEON BRITTAN, QC
Vice-President of the European Commission

CAMBRIDGE
GROTIUS PUBLICATIONS LIMITED
1991

SALES & GROTIUS PUBLICATIONS LTD.
ADMINISTRATION PO BOX 115, CAMBRIDGE, CB3 9BP,
ENGLAND.

British Library Cataloguing in Publication Data

Brittan, Leon, 1939–
    Competition policy and merger control in the single
    European market. — (Hersch Lauterpacht memorial
    lectures; 10)
    I. Title II. Series
    342.66626094

ISBN 0-949009-92-X

©
GROTIUS PUBLICATIONS LIMITED
1991

Typeset and printed by
Black Bear Press Limited, Cambridge

COMPETITION POLICY
AND MERGER CONTROL IN
THE SINGLE EUROPEAN MARKET

Titles published in the Hersch Lauterpacht Memorial Lecture Series

CONTENTS

PREFACE

I was deeply touched and greatly honoured to be asked to deliver these lectures. When I went up to Cambridge as an undergraduate Sir Hersch Lauterpacht was already a legendary figure in his lifetime. But the true extent of the regard and affection in which he was held in the world of international law and beyond was most vividly brought home to me on his death, when an unforgettable stream of distinguished figures from far and near came specially to Cambridge to pay their last respects to him.

I sadly never knew Sir Hersch personally, but his son Eli Lauterpacht, QC taught me international law at Cambridge and thirty years later invited me to give these lectures.

I have enormously enjoyed both giving them and subsequently having the opportunity of discussing some of the ideas in them with members of the Cambridge international law community. Preparing the lectures helped me to clarify my own thoughts and has also greatly stimulated my further thinking in this area since then.

Even in the short time since the lectures were delivered much has happened in European Community competition law. The Merger Regulation came into effect in September 1990 and since then the steady stream of cases has already led us in the Commission to give our first interpretations of the text of the Regulation: to begin filling in some of the interstices. In addition some notable cases have enabled us to use competition law in a constructive way, and not merely as a policing operation, for example by extending choice for the consumer and opportunities for operators in the aviation industry.

Above all, however, the last year has reinforced my belief that it is necessary to extend co-operation in competition law on an international basis. Negotiations between the European Community and the United States in this area are now well under way. Looking further ahead, it is becoming increasingly clear that if market opportunities are to continue to be extended, international negotiations will increasingly have to cover competition issues and not just trade issues. For the readiness to accept other people's goods and services will more and more depend on having confidence that a broadly comparable competition policy is being followed by one's trading partners.

All of this is food for much future thought and work. For the moment let me conclude by expressing my warmest thanks to a distinguished member of my Brussels team, Jonathan Faull, for his unstinting assistance with these lectures. His deep knowledge and understanding of European Community competition law has been an inestimable and indeed indispensable help in all my work at the Commission in this field – but nowhere more than in the preparation of these lectures.

Leon Brittan

Brussels
January 1991

TABLE OF CASES

ABBREVIATIONS

A.C.	Appeal Cases
A.J.I.L.	American Journal of International Law
B.Y.I.L.	British Yearbook of International Law
C.M.L.R.	Common Market Law Reports
DG IV	Directorate-General of Competition, Commission of the European Communities
E.C.R.	European Court Reports
EFTA	European Free Trade Association
Eur. Intell. Prop. Rev.	European Intellectual Property Review
I.C.J. Rep.	International Court of Justice Reports
I.C.L.Q.	International and Comparative Law Quarterly
J.	*Clunet*
J.O.	Journal Officiel des Communautés Européennes
O.J.	Official Journal of the European Communities
P.C.I.J.	Permanent Court of International Justice

PART I

JURISDICTIONAL ISSUES IN EEC COMPETITION LAW

It is a great privilege to be invited to deliver these lectures in honour of so distinguished a jurist, Sir Hersch Lauterpacht. I speak to you as a lawyer by training, a politician by calling and one who now finds himself at the heart of one of the most important developments in international law *and* politics of this century: the European Community. The Community's legal order was born in Treaties between sovereign States governed by international law; yet today it is no longer particularly controversial to note that Community law has transcended its international law origins and operates in many ways like municipal law, creating and regulating rights and obligations in the fields in which the Member States have pooled their sovereignty. I cannot help feeling that Sir Hersch Lauterpacht would feel completely at home with this development. On the other hand, he might be impatient with my suggestion that Community law has transcended international law: and perhaps what we are really seeing in the Community is the operation of international law as it should actually be. Professor Feinberg commented on Sir Hersch Lauterpacht that

> Two main subjects engaged his attention throughout his life. One was advancement of the integration of the international Community by restricting sovereignty and imposing the rule of law and justice on international life and relations. The other was the honouring of human rights and fundamental freedoms and their protection through international law.[1]

This seems to me to encapsulate the ideals which we are seeking to pursue in the European Community. My subject in this lecture may serve to highlight one particular aspect of the Community's manifold endeavours. Simply put, the question

[1] Feinberg, "Hersch Lauterpacht – Jurist and Thinker" in *Studies in International Law*, Jerusalem, 1979, 213, 219.

is: to what extent may the Community's competition rules be applied to companies, persons and activities outside its territory? This is a matter of Community law and a matter of international law. It is also, I say directly and with no apology, a matter of politics.

I intend to focus primarily on legislative or prescriptive jurisdiction, although I shall touch on enforcement jurisdiction as well. By legislative or prescriptive jurisdiction I mean the power of a State to make and apply substantive rules. What interests me in particular is the power of the European Community (which is for present purposes the equivalent of a State) to apply its competition rules, mainly Articles 85 and 86 of the Treaty of Rome, to restrictive practices with a foreign element. I shall eschew the word "extra-territorial" because it is often wrongly used, frequently begs the question I wish to discuss and seems to be one of those legal words which become terms of pejorative art.[2]

I know that there has long been a debate in international law about whether States have unlimited jurisdiction except where international law specifically provides otherwise or whether they may act only in compliance with international law generally at least outside the domestic sphere. The debate about jurisdiction in competition matters of course raises this issue. In my view, States may exercise jurisdiction in competition cases with a foreign element only to the extent permitted by international law. The State as a subject of international law is a repository of rights and duties created by international law. This is more obviously true of the European Community, a creature of international law and bound by its

---

[2] See Bischoff and Kovar, "L'application du droit communautaire de la concurrence aux entreprises établies à l'extérieur de la Communauté". 102 J. 75, 675, note 3: "Il est des mots qui, dans le langage juridique, comportent une condamnation implicite..."; Ferry, "Towards completing the charm: the Woodpulp judgment", [1989] Eur. Intell. Prop. Rev., 19, 20: "a certain lack of intellectual rigour has accorded to the term 'extra-territorial jurisdiction' an emotive content"; Hawk, *United States, Common Market and International Antitrust: A Comparative Guide*, 2nd ed., revised 1989, Vol. I, 65: "The term "extraterritorial" has caused far more heat than light in the debate about the appropriate limits of

rules which has grown into an actor in its own right on the world stage. Nevertheless, whatever view one takes of the nature of the State in international law, the jurisdictional problem facing the Community is the same: how far can Articles 85 and 86 be applied to cases with a foreign element without falling foul of international law?

Although the nature of competition law presents a difficult problem of classification, perhaps the most realistic response is to see it as a *sui generis* body of economic law, sometimes part of criminal law and sometimes civil, sometimes enforced by public prosecution, sometimes a cause of action in litigation between private parties, sometimes a sword in an action for damages, sometimes a shield in a breach of contract suit.

A learned specialist in this field has sought to distinguish between the jurisdictional reach of various types of antitrust proceedings.[3] However, it seems to me more satisfactory that there should be one rule governing the reach of the substantive provisions of the Community's competition law, wherever and by whomsoever enforcement is undertaken. As far as Community law is concerned, enforcement by the Commission of the Treaty's competition rules by the imposition of fines pursuant to the Council's implementing Regulations is not regarded as penal[4] and, unless this is obviously wrong or deceitful, *quod non*, international law should respect its subject's classification.

It seems to be generally agreed that the key to the jurisdictional reach of competition rules is the precise extent and qualification of the territorial principle. Other principles of jurisdiction – protection, passive personality, universality – have no or limited application to competition law. But the

antitrust laws in international trade". Hawk's work contains an extensive set of materials on this issue.

[3] Akehurst, "Jurisdiction in International Law", XLVI B.Y.I.L. (1972-3) 145, 190-2.

[4] See Council Regulations 17/62, Art. 15(4); 1017/68, Art. 22(4); 4056/85, Art. 19(4); 3975/87, Art. 12(4); and most recently 4064/89 (the merger Regulation), Art. 14(4).

nationality principle does enable a State to regulate the activities of its citizens and, by extension, of companies incorporated within its borders, wherever those activities are carried out or have effects. Competition law, however, is concerned with markets and is not usually applied to deal with the activities abroad of one's own companies. But, it may be said, if competition is seen as a guiding principle of economic life, one may wish to stop one's companies entering into cartels anywhere, if only to fend off any habit-forming tendencies. On the other hand, some States may seek to encourage co-operation by positively authorizing certain types of apparently anti-competitive conduct: our own Article 85(3) and the US Webb-Pomerene Act are obvious examples. We cannot seriously expect the authorities in our export markets to stand back and bless these authorized activities merely because we have exercised our jurisdiction. Competition law should be applied only in order to deal with competition issues in one's own market and not to make sure that one's own companies behave in a certain way abroad. Competition law is essentially territorial in scope.

The main problem of the application of the territorial principle lies in establishing what must take place within the territory to engage jurisdiction. Is it all the conduct complained of, some of it, a constituent element of it or its effect? If any of those nouns is the right one, what qualifying adjectives should be added to it?

Article 3(f) of the Treaty of Rome provides that the Community's activities shall include "the institution of a system ensuring that competition in the common market is not distorted".

This provision has quasi-Constitutional status as a binding principle guiding the Community's endeavours. It is given concrete expression in the two basic substantive competition Articles 85 and 86.

Article 85 contains two expressions which have a juris-dictional ring about them for a lawyer: a restrictive practice is caught by Article 85(1) if it "may affect trade between Member States" and has as its "object in effect the prevention, restriction or distortion of competition within the common market". Article 86 also contains two notions which suggest themselves as jurisdictional: the abuse must be of a dominant position "within the common market or in a substantial part of it" and is prohibited "in so far as it may affect trade between Member States".

The notion of "effect on trade between Member States" common to Articles 85 and 86 engages Community jurisdiction alongside the possible application of the competition laws of the Member States. It tells us little about the limitations which Community law provides in respect of its jurisdiction vis-à-vis foreign companies or States.

Articles 85 and 86 both require that something should happen "within the common market", although in the case of Article 85 the impact on competition there may be the object or the effect of the agreement, concerted practice or decision in question. The fundamental scope of Community competition law is therefore territorial. This is not surprising since its purpose is to provide for a competitive domestic market (Article 3(f)). It would no doubt be an attractive proposition to have competitive markets elsewhere too, but this is properly a matter for persuasion, example and international relations. I might add that recent events in Europe beyond the Community's borders suggest that the virtues and benefits of competition in our market have not gone unnoticed.

The scope of the Community's competition law, then, is territorial. That is easy enough to state. The problems start when competition within the territory is affected by someone or something with a foreign element. This could be, for example, an agreement where some or all of the parties have their manufacturing facilities outside the Community or simply an agreement concluded in a foreign country under the law of that country. If such an agreement has or is liable to have an effect on prices, supplies or output in the Community, the Commission must have regard to its duty to create and preserve a system of undistorted competition. The European consumer and his or her elected representatives want to see us carrying out our duty and are unlikely to be impressed by the argument that high prices or restricted supplies are caused by foreign companies or agreements signed beyond our borders about which we can do nothing.

What then can we do and what have we been doing? Let me reassure all European consumers right away that there is a considerable body of case law which shows that we have been very active in prohibiting and punishing anti-competitive behaviour over the years and have dealt fairly and without discrimination with all sorts of companies from within and outside the Community. I shall mention some of the leading cases to illustrate this. Controversy has by and large been avoided by our responsible approach and scrupulous compliance with OECD recommendations and other bilateral international arrangements. Let us look now at the cases, remembering that the closer we come to espousal of the "effects doctrine" the more controversial the question of jurisdiction becomes. I do not propose to delve into the detail of every Commission decision and Court judgment with a bearing on this matter. I shall attempt rather to identify and illustrate certain trends in the development of Community law, culminating in the position today and then looking at future prospects.

The Court of Justice held in 1971[5] in the *Béguelin* case that the fact that one of the parties to an agreement falling under Article 85(1) was situated outside the Community did not prevent that provision from applying if the agreement is "operative" ("*produit ses effets*") on the territory of the common market. Argument quickly broke out about how *obiter* the relevant *dictum* was and whether or not this constituted an endorsement of the (or indeed an) effects doctrine. I am content to note that the judgment made clear that the location of a party's place of incorporation or headquarters is immaterial for competition law, which is and must be concerned with impact on markets. Professor Mann may have

---

[5] Case 22/71, *Béguelin Import Co.* v. *GL Import-Export S.A.*, [1971] E.C.R. 949, [1972] C.M.L.R. 81.

been right to say that the judgment cannot be treated as "the source of a legal rule of great width and impact",[6] but it was certainly an important step in clearing the way for the development of a sensible approach to jurisdiction. Anticipating a little, I would say that corporate and geographical veils had to be lifted and *Béguelin* was a good start.

Since then there have been many decisions and judgments applying the competition rules to foreign companies and the issue has largely ceased to be controversial. It is noteworthy that, in the 1987 case involving the acquisition by Philip Morris of shares in the Rothmans group from Rembrandt, many legal issues were raised but not the relevance to Articles 85 and 86 of the fact that the purchaser was American and the vendor South African. Jurisdictional questions were paramount in the German proceedings in the same case, but not in the proceedings before the Commission or the European Court of Justice.[7]

Meanwhile, Community competition law had developed or rather rejected another doctrine: we do not generally have what the Americans call the "intra-enterprise conspiracy".[8]

For Article 85(1) to apply, there must be two or more undertakings involved. Early Commission decisions held that Article 85(1) did not apply to arrangements between parent and subsidiary within a group of companies. The Court of Justice has had to consider this issue in a number of cases and has laid down what is called the economic unit doctrine, whereby an "undertaking" for the purposes of Articles 85 and 86 "must be understood as designating an economic unit ... even if in law that economic unit consists of several persons,

---

[6] "The Dyestuffs Case in the Court of Justice of the European Communities", 22 I.C.L.Q. (1973) 48, 49.

[7] Cases 142 and 156/84, *British-American Tobacco and R.J. Reynolds* v. *Commission*, [1987] E.C.R. 4487.

[8] In the USA, the intra-enterprise or "bathtub" conspiracy has had a chequered career. The leading recent judgment of the Supreme Court in *Copperweld Corp.* v. *Independence Tube Corp.*, 467 U.S. 752 (1984) held that relations between a parent company and its wholly owned subsidiary are not subject to antitrust liability. See Hawk, pp. 292.2-300.

legal or natural".[9] The group formed by parent and subsidiary or subsidiaries is not a plurality of undertakings: it *is* an undertaking. It may not, therefore, fall foul of Article 85 in respect of its internal arrangements, but it may abuse a dominant position within the meaning of Article 86 since that provision applies to the activities of "one or more under-takings". However, the most important consequence of the economic unit doctrine for present purposes is its application to bring foreign parts of the unit under the Community's jurisdiction and to impute behaviour from one part of the unit to another. Here too the case law is abundant and I do not wish to take time in tracing its development. Suffice it to say that the presence of a subsidiary within the Community brings the whole group into our jurisdiction for the service of papers and other enforcement measures, while the activities in the Community of a group with a subsidiary in its territory fall within our jurisdiction even if the activities concerned are ostensibly carried out or instigated by the parent company elsewhere. The *locus classicus* is the *Dyestuffs* case[10] where the Commission had to deal with a concerted practice to raise prices for aniline dyes involving several producers including one British and two Swiss companies which claimed to be outside the Community's jurisdiction. The Commission and the learned Advocate General Mr Mayras founded jurisdic-tion on the effects doctrine. Mr Mayras's opinion contains a masterly survey of the law as it stood at the time and he recommended that the Court endorse as compatible with international law the doctrine that direct, immediate and substantial effects within the Community's territory of an act committed abroad are sufficient to engage jurisdiction under Article 85. However, the Commission in its pleadings before the Court had suggested that the economic unit doctrine be used as an alternative basis for jurisdiction. The Court of

[9] Case 170/83, *Hydrotherm* v. *Compact*, [1984] E.C.R. 2999, 3016, [1985] 3 C.M.L.R. 224.
[10] Commission decision J.O. 1969 L 195/11, [1969] C.M.L.R. D23; Court of Justice Case 48/69, *I.C.I.* v. *Commission*, [1972] E.C.R. 619; Case 52/69, *Geigy* v. *Commission*, [1972] E.C.R. 787; Case 53/69, *Sandoz* v. *Commission*, [1972] E.C.R. 845.

Justice, which also had before it a closely argued and strongly worded Aide-Mémoire presented by the British Government to the Commission against the effects doctrine, did not endorse that doctrine at all. It upheld the Commission's decision on the basis of the economic unit theory. The foreign companies operated in the Community by means of subsidiaries – indeed their price rises were effected through subsidiaries. The foreign parents were therefore acting in the Community and had to submit to its jurisdiction. It was not necessary to consider whether account could be taken of the effects of the offence within the territory, since both the offender and the offence were themselves located in the territory.

Subsequently, much debate and refinement has taken place on such issues as the extension of the parent – wholly owned subsidiary definition of a group to other networks of relationships: controlled subsidiaries, branches, agents, etc. The message, however, was clear: the corporate veil was no protection for a foreigner doing business in the Community through some emanation or entity which formed a group of which it was a constituent part. The group is the undertaking.

There seems to be an inexorable rule of case law development that, sooner or later, the hard case must be faced which poses the unambiguous question which a previous generation was able not to answer in deciding a slightly less hard case in a different way. For many years one wondered what would happen when a case arose under Article 85 involving foreign companies selling into the Community without any presence in its territory whatsoever. In 1984 the Commission considered two cases which seemed to raise the effects question. The first concerned imports of aluminium into the Community[11] and involved, amongst others, undertakings from Eastern Europe apparently unrepresented in the Community, making direct sales into it from without. The Commission asserted jurisdiction on the basis of the effects of the restriction of competition within the Community and held

[11] *Aluminium Imports from Eastern Europe*, O.J. 1985 L 92.

that there was no rule of international law which prevented it from doing so. There was no appeal against the Commission's decision. On the same day as it took the *Aluminium* decision, the Commission issued a decision in the *Wood Pulp* case.[12] This involved a concerted practice between North American, Scandinavian, Portuguese and Spanish pulp producers to restrict price competition in the Community market. There were appeals against the Commission's decision and, while the case is still pending on the substance of the decision under Article 85, the Court of Justice has already delivered judgment on the preliminary issue of jurisdiction.[13] The Commission's decision found that only some of the parties had branches, subsidiaries, agencies or other establishments within the Community and based its jurisdiction on the effects doctrine. Indeed it explained in its fourteenth report on competition policy[14] that "the *Aluminium* and *Wood Pulp* cases illustrate the Commission's assumption of jurisdiction over non-EEC undertakings when the activities of those undertakings have a direct and appreciable effect on competition and trade within the EEC. This reflects the policy, which is essential in view of the realities of modern world trade, that all undertakings doing business within the EEC must respect the rules of competition in the same way, regardless of their place of establishment ('effects doctrine')."

In the *Wood Pulp* case before the Court of Justice, the *Dyestuffs* pattern of events seemed to repeat itself: the Commission took a firm decision espousing the effects doctrine, but offered an alternative in its pleadings in the Court of Justice; the United Kingdom intervened as *amicus curiae* against the effects doctrine; the Advocate-General

---

[12] O.J. 1985 L 26.

[13] Cases 89/85, etc. *Åhlström et al.* v. *Commission*, [1988] E.C.R. 5193, [1988] 4 C.M.L.R. 901. There have already been learned commentaries on the judgment and there are no doubt many more to come: see, for example, Ferry, loc. cit.; Van Gerven, "EC jurisdiction in antitrust matters: the Wood Pulp judgment", 1989 Fordham Corporate Law Institute (1990), 451.

[14] Brussels/Luxembourg, 1985, p. 59.

endorsed that doctrine; the Court of Justice found another basis for jurisdiction.

It is with the Court's judgment that I propose to deal since it is the latest judicial pronouncement in Community law on the status of the effects doctrine. Or rather it is not, because the Court ignored the doctrine and proceeded to establish jurisdiction in another way. The Commission had found that the parties were either "exporting directly to or doing business within the Community", thus distinguishing between acting outside the territory by selling into it and presence within the territory by means of representation or having fellow group-members in the territory. The Commission claimed jurisdiction over both categories and, in the former case, invoked the effects doctrine: "the effect of the agreements and practices on prices announced and charged to customers and on resale of pulp within the EEC was ... not only substantial but intended and was the primary and direct result of the agreements and practices".

The Court first considered the terms of Article 85(1) and found on the facts that the Commission had applied that provision correctly as regards its territorial scope. Only then did the Court turn to consider whether the Commission's application of Article 85 complied with international law. The Court examined the constituent elements of a violation of Article 85. In so doing, it no doubt had in mind the celebrated judgment of the Permanent Court of International Justice in the *Lotus* case[15] in which the majority opinion endorsed the effects doctrine in relation to crime where the effect, a constituent element of the offence, took place in the territory of the State claiming jurisdiction. To extrapolate and simplify considerably, does a crime take place where the trigger is pulled or where the bullet kills the victim? Does a competition offence take place where it is agreed to raise prices or where goods at those prices are actually sold? The Court of Justice answers: both. An agreement which infringes Article 85 consists of conduct made up of two elements: the formation of

[15] P.C.I.J. Ser. A, No. 10 (1927), 1.

the agreement and its implementation. Jurisdiction over conduct cannot depend solely on the place of formation of the agreement because undertakings cannot be given such an easy way of escaping their responsibilities. In other words, international law cannot be supposed to contain a rule which makes a mockery of a respectable provision of municipal law, depriving it of its "*effet utile*". So the second element, the place of implementation, must be decisive. It was immaterial whether or not the parties had recourse to subsidiaries, agents, sub-agents or branches within the Community in order to make contracts with purchasers and the argument of fact on this point was thus disposed of. Selling directly into the Community at prices agreed outside it was an *implementation* in the Community of the agreement formed elsewhere. There was therefore conduct within the Community and there could be no question of extra-territorial jurisdiction. "The Community's jurisdiction to apply its rules to such conduct", said the Court, "is covered by the territoriality principle as universally recognized in public international law". This reasonable approach rightly places competition law in its proper context: that of keeping markets competitive. A market-related law cannot be made to depend on form and accident (or even choice) of location: it is the impact on prices in the market which counts. Many, indeed an increasing number of States have competition laws and it is to denigrate international law to suggest that it prevents proper application of those laws by enabling defendants to hide behind corporate veils and geographical frontiers. The real problem, as I shall explain shortly, is one of politics and diplomacy: how to cope with the coexistence of different national laws and policies in this area. But before that, you will want to know whether the mystery story of the effects doctrine has a conclusion or not. The fundamental question is: does implementation which the Court regarded as the touchstone, mean or include effects? No-one may expect a court to establish a new, legal principle if there is another, less controversial way of deciding a case before it. Nor may one lightly accuse a court of establishing the more controversial principle by presenting it in less controversial or at least more ambiguous clothing. The learned Advocate-General in the *Wood Pulp* case, Mr Darmon, developed at length the qualifications to be attached to the notion of effects, as his predecessor Mr Mayras had done previously in the *Dyestuffs* case. The Court did not consider the qualifications and it is in my view unreasonable to assume unqualified espousal of a doctrine in a judgment which does not mention it by name while those who urged its adoption accepted that it should be qualified. So the Court of Justice did not endorse the effects doctrine. The only way to resolve the issue is to see whether there is a genuine difference between the concept of "implementation" and that of "effects". Is there any kind of anti-competitive conduct liable to fall under Article 85 whose effects are different from its implementation? If so, there is still one more hurdle which the Court may or may not wish to jump when the ultimate hard case in this area eventually comes its way.

Are there circumstances in which there is no implementation, but there is an effect? It has been suggested that the sale by a foreign producer of its goods direct to Community purchasers or through independent distributors doing business on their own behalf should not be characterized as "implementing conduct" because many States would be able to exercise jurisdiction over the same conduct.[16] But the Court of Justice held that the sale in the Community at the concerted price *was* an implementation and I find that conclusion thoroughly reasonable and appropriate in the light of competition law's purposes and territorial scope. Nevertheless, this specific use of the word "implementation" rather than "effects" suggests to me that implementing conduct perhaps has to be direct, substantial and foreseeable for jurisdiction to be engaged. It is clear, however, that the sale of goods into the Community at prices determined by collusion between producers elsewhere must engage our jurisdiction. Indeed, I would find it hard to do my job of ensuring that the common market is based on a system of undistorted

---

[16] Van Gerven, op. cit., p. 470.

competition to the full if it were otherwise. Rather than deny jurisdiction, if this is the case, we should seek better rules for consultation and avoidance and, if need be, resolution of disputes brought about by the exercise of conflicting jurisdictions.

The most telling argument in favour of the view that there can be effect without implementation is that an agreement not to do something or, in Article 86 terms, a refusal to supply by an undertaking in a dominant position cannot properly be described as implementing conduct at all.[17] For example, (i) in the *Wood Pulp* case, the parties might have agreed to share markets world-wide, with some undertaking not to export to the Community at all (or perhaps, I would add, to refine further this hypothesis, not below a certain price). Have parties implemented an agreement within the Community when they simply refuse to sell to a purchaser there because of the terms of the agreement? (ii) Supposing US, Japanese and British stock exchange dealers agree to rig a market by not doing something in London; is omission implementing conduct? (iii) If all the *Wood Pulp* producers divided the EC market between them and agreed to sell FOB only, making no attempt to market within the Community, where is the conduct inside the Community if one producer refused to supply to another's area?[18]

Advocate-General van Gerven in his paper on *Wood Pulp*[19] makes a fascinating argument based on the language and purpose of the Community's competition rules for the jurisdictional criterion of "appreciable effect on the competitive conditions of the market" which, he says, is in full compliance with international law. He integrates into one criterion the various theories of jurisdiction so far used in Community law and shows proper regard for the structural approach of the community competition rules and their market integration objective.

[17] See, e.g. Van Gerven, p. 471 and Ferry, loc. cit.
[18] The examples are taken from Ferry, p. 22.
[19] Van Gerven, pp. 473-4.

You will appreciate my reluctance to speculate about possible future case law developments. Whether conduct includes not doing something is not an issue which can be resolved in the Community context by one dictionary, one philosophy or one legal system. It will depend on the Court of Justice's perception of the law and the facts of the case before it in the circumstances of the Community at the time. If the implementation doctrine falls short of the full effects doctrine, in my view both may be seen as legitimate expressions of the territoriality principle and it may be that one day a case will arise in which only the full effects doctrine will enable the Community's competition rules to be applied properly. The Court of Justice will then have to consider, indeed reconsider, the issues in the light of Community law and international law. Let us return from the realm of legal speculation to the world of practical politics. We have in the Community a legal system which contains a commitment to competition policy. We even like to think that it is part of the Community's constitutional order. Many countries share a similar commitment and have enacted laws to protect competition in their markets. We live in an increasingly interdependent world in which economic activities do not stop and start again at national borders. When you add the remark made by Lord Wilberforce that "it is axiomatic that in antitrust matters the policy of one state may be to defend what it is the policy of another state to attack",[20] it is obvious that we have a recipe for conflict, but also every interest in devising solutions.

Modern juridical writings and some state practice point to the development of principles of international law to limit the way in which territorial jurisdiction in its various guises and extensions is exercised in competition matters. The European Court of Justice considered two such principles in the *Wood Pulp* case: non-interference and comity.

The principle of non-interference would prohibit a state from applying its law if the regulatory interests which it is

---

[20] *In re Westinghouse Electric Corporation Uranium Contract Litigation*, [1978] A.C. 547, 617.

pursuing are outweighed by the interests of a foreign state likely to be seriously injured by the measures to be taken under the law concerned. Quite apart from the practical difficulties of applying such a principle, it is not certain that it has yet hardened into a rule of international law. The Court of Justice in *Wood Pulp* held that it was not necessary to determine whether the rule existed because, even if it did, the Commission had not breached it. The actual claim made by some of the parties was that they were being made subject to contradictory rules; in fact, Article 85 told them not to behave like a cartel in the EEC, while the US Webb-Pomerene Act merely exempted them from US antitrust liability: there was clearly no contradiction, no clash.

If the principle of non-interference is not a rule of international law, it may be a species of *comity*. Comity itself is more a principle than a rule. The US Supreme Court defined it in 1987 as referring to "the spirit of cooperation in which a domestic tribunal approaches the resolution of cases touching the laws and interests of other sovereign states".[21] I see comity as an expression of the obligations of States to exercise moderation and restraint in exercising jurisdiction in cases with a foreign element and to take due account of the law and interests of other States in such cases. If such moderation extends to the avoidance of "undue encroachment on a jurisdiction more properly appertaining to, or more appropriately exercisable by, another state",[22] we are very close to non-interference.

In any case, the Commission does consider itself obliged to have regard to comity when exercising its jurisdiction in competition cases with a foreign element. We respect scrupulously the relevant OECD recommendations and consider foreign States' interests and observations in a wide network of bilateral and other contacts. In addition, the Commission as a

---

[21] *Aérospatiale* v. *U.S. District Court for the Southern District of Iowa*, 482 U.S. 522 (1987).

[22] See Sir Gerald Fitzmaurice's Separate Opinion in *Barcelona Traction*, [1970] I.C.J. Rep. 65, 105.

collegiate body does not have to consult another department or branch of government to ascertain the likely impact of a proposed course of action on the Community's external relations. A Commission decision on competition policy reflects the totality of the Commission's views and policies. My colleague in charge of external relations sits near me in Commission when decisions are taken and his department talks to mine.

Other suggestions have been made of appropriate ways to deal with the problems I have been discussing. Let me mention two of them. In the United States, interplay between the courts, learned writers and the Restatement procedure has produced a number of related ideas involving interest balancing and a jurisdictional rule of reason.[23] Professor Mann's "contacts" approach seeks points of contact between a set of facts and a state which are "so close, so substantial, so direct, so weighty, that legislation in respect of them is in harmony with international law and its various aspects".[24] If self-restraint and due regard for the interests of others are proper limits on the *exercise* of our jurisdiction, the principles of "reasonableness"[25] as it is put in the US and "proportionality" in Community law can help guide us to proper respect for comity between nations.

The principles discussed above are shared to a very large extent by the Community's major trading partners and actual confrontations are rare. It is indeed true, as a learned specialist in this field has pointed out, that "there are more proposed solutions to the problem of international antitrust conflicts than there are individual cases creating those conflicts".[26] I have no desire to offer solutions to problems which are non-existent, rare or usually solved anyway. The

---

[23] See generally Advocate-General Darmon in *Wood Pulp*; B. Hawk, op. cit., Vol. I.

[24] 111 Recueil des Cours (1964), 49. See Advocate General Van Gerven, loc. cit.

[25] Fox, "Extraterritoriality and Antitrust – Is 'Reasonableness' the answer?", 1986 Fordham Corporate Law Institute (1987).

[26] Hawk, op. cit., Vol. I-A, p. 800.

reason for my interest in this issue is, however, more than academic.

The world in which business operates is characterized by falling barriers and integration of markets. In the European Community, the single internal market is within our grasp. In our relations with EFTA countries today, and perhaps with other European countries tomorrow, our markets are coming together and we are searching for rules and mechanisms to reflect the new realities, in the competition area and elsewhere. Looking further afield, there is a growing perception that EC-US relations should be put on a more formal footing. In the US, there are signs that more active antitrust enforcement may be expected from the Bush administration. In the Community, the commitment to competition policy has never been stronger, as is shown by the unanimous adoption by the Council of Ministers in December 1989 of a Regulation giving the Commission long-awaited merger control responsibilities. With the best will in the world, to take the most likely example, the US and the Community may well one day soon take different views of a competition case. It could be a merger between two US car producers active in Europe or it could be the other way round. It is not difficult to think of hypothetical cases, but I do not wish to give hostages to fortune or to encourage speculation. If it is not the US, it will be Switzerland or Sweden, Canada, Australia or Japan. It is difficult to believe that the rather general rules and principles that I have just been discussing will be sufficient in themselves to ensure that different jurisdictions come to the same conclusion about the same case. The problem cases may be rare now, but they will increase in number and complexity.

Before outlining possible ways forward, one should not forget that there is more to jurisdiction than making rules. Enforcing competition law involves such matters as obtaining information, sometimes by compulsion, ordering companies to cease and desist, imposing remedies which in merger cases may include partial or total divestiture and the levying of fines and penalties. The Commission's practice is to exercise enforcement jurisdiction in all cases where it has prescriptive jurisdiction. However, we always seek to limit possible difficulties by informing foreign authorities of our activities and by complying with their wishes whenever possible. We do not send inspectors into company premises outside the Community and have not yet had to seek payment of a fine outside our territory. Common sense, compliance with OECD recommendations and the nature of our bilateral relations with countries which share our commitment to the legal and policy requirements discussed above have enabled us to avoid confrontation. But here again, something more may be needed in our changing world. The Community has at present a series of bilateral agreements with foreign countries providing for comparable competition rules and consultation mechanisms. We are also, quite willingly, subject to recommendations made in the OECD and other international bodies. The Commission enjoys regular contacts with competition authorities all over the world. Nonetheless something more specific has been happening around us. Largely because of fears of the US exercise of jurisdiction in respect of issues with a foreign element, several countries have enacted so-called "blocking statutes". South Africa, Australia, the United Kingdom, France and Canada all have legislation in response to US enforcement of antitrust and other laws. While these statutes differ in scope and content, their purpose is to protect companies from the long arm of foreign law enforcement, usually in respect of the production of documents and other discovery procedures. Probably the most celebrated antitrust case is the *Laker* saga. Introducing the British Protection of Trading Interests Bill, the Minister responsible referred to Winston Churchill's famous remark that jaw-jaw is better than war-war and said that "for years we tried jaw-jaw. We have now been driven to law-law."[27] This summed up the feelings of frustration felt in many countries about US legal forays overseas.

However, a more positive development has been the conclusion of international agreements between the US and

[27] Hansard, 15 November 1979, cols. 1591-2.

foreign countries on antitrust matters. While there were frequently clauses in Treaties of Friendship, Commerce and Navigation between the US and other countries providing for consultations to eliminate the harmful effects of restrictive business practices in trade between them, this did not solve the problem of perceived extraterritoriality. Indeed, the State Department stated in 1980 that "FCN Treaties do not constrain the United States from the exercise of extraterritorial jurisdiction that would otherwise be permissible".[28] Specific antitrust Treaties have, however, now been concluded between the US and the Federal Republic of Germany (1976), Australia (1982) and Canada (1984). Within the European Community, France and Germany signed an agreement in 1984. These Treaties go under various names and make different provisions for different problems. I do not suggest that any one of them should be taken as a model. What they all have in common is a desire to cooperate and avoid confrontation, and an enthusiasm for bringing this about coupled with a properly jealous regard for each side's prerogatives and responsibilities.

As the Community moves with confidence and determination towards the completion of its single market, its competition policy is busy filling in gaps so that it may adopt a comprehensive approach to business life in the new market. This inevitably means that our problems become more international in scope. As we come to grips with air and sea transport, international mergers, telecommunications networks, energy supplies and industry-wide cartels, we realize just how far our horizons stretch. Competition policy has come of age and must face up to the challenges of our interdependent world. One of these is to provide for rapid consultation procedures and dispute avoidance mechanisms in competition matters with our major trading partners.

I personally favour, to start with, a treaty between the European Community and the United States. It would provide for consultations, exchanges of non-confidential

[28] 74 A.J.I.L. 667 (1980), cited in Hawk, op. cit., Vol. I-A, p. 738, n. 544.

information, mutual assistance, and best endeavours to cooperate in enforcement where policies coincide and to resolve disputes where they do not. Disagreements should be discussed frankly and, wherever possible, only one party should exercise jurisdiction over the same set of facts. To make that possible, a party with jurisdiction should be ready not to exercise it in certain defined circumstances, while the other party, in its exercise of jurisdiction, should agree to take full account of the interests and views of its partner. If the parties do exercise jurisdiction concurrently, they should both take account of each other's concerns and seek to adapt remedies accordingly. We have to accept that there will be scenarios, I hope rare, where even if the Treaty is applied in good faith, no agreement will be reached. Arbitration is a possibility, but I find it hard to believe that the US or the EC would be willing to give up the opportunity of having the last word about fundamental aspects of market behaviour and structure in their respective territories.

It is too early to say precisely what might be achieved by EC-US negotiations. Talks are under way and are proving encouraging. It is equally impossible to predict the impact of an EC-US treaty on international law and relations generally in this field, although I would expect its impact to be considerable and positive.

The EC-US treaty would almost certainly be limited to enforcement by public authorities. The many legal issues raised by litigation in courts in the US and the Community are likely to prove too complex at this stage.

To conclude, therefore, I consider that a combination of proper respect for international law, politically responsible exercise of self-restraint and regard for others and comprehensive bilateral treaties between the free market world's trading powers is what is needed to provide a framework for the application of competition law in today's environment. We do not have much time, as the internationalization of business is taking place rapidly. We in the Commission are ready to meet the challenge.

PART II

THE DEVELOPMENT OF MERGER CONTROL IN EEC COMPETITION LAW

A. THE DEVELOPMENT OF MERGER CONTROL IN EEC COMPETITION LAW

In this lecture, I propose to focus on merger control in the European Economic Community, although it should not be forgotten that a comprehensive Community system of merger control has existed in the European Coal and Steel Community since its inception. The EEC is of more topical interest because of the adoption of Council Regulation No. 4064/89[1] on the control of concentrations between undertakings on 21 December 1989. The EEC also covers a vast range of economic sectors, whereas the ECSC Treaty is necessarily limited in scope.

Before explaining the genesis of the new Regulation and its legal and policy implications, one must first consider the history of the European Communities and ask why the ECSC Treaty contained detailed rules on mergers, whereas the EEC Treaty did not. The Treaty of Paris, which created the ECSC, was signed in 1951 and entered into force in 1952 for a period of fifty years. It was rooted in the experience of the Second World War and symbolized Franco-German reconciliation by bringing together the key industries of the time under a supranational umbrella. Coal and steel were seen to have played an important part in the preparation and conduct of the war and also to have a crucial role to play in the economic reconstruction of Europe. The re-emergence of cartels, trusts, oligopolies, concentrations and dominant market positions was a genuine fear and the brave decision was taken by the six founding Member States to entrust the High Authority, now

---

[1] O.J. L257/13 (21 September 1990). A convenient compendium of the Regulation and related texts has been published as a Supplement to the Bulletin of the European Communities (No. 2/90).

the Commission, with considerable powers in the competition field. Indeed, as regards mergers, the High Authority was given exclusive jurisdiction throughout the Community and wide-ranging powers to do the job properly.

Then in 1958, the Treaty of Rome set up the European Economic Community and the words merger and concentration were nowhere to be found. Although examination of the 1956 Spaak Report does indicate that the problem of the anti-competitive consequences of dominant positions and monopolization was not ignored, it must be said that the merger issue was not high on anyone's agenda in Europe in the mid-1950s. National competition policy, where it existed, was not overly concerned with mergers and the EEC's founding Treaty reflected that situation. So we were left with Article 85 on restrictive practices and agreements and Article 86 on abuses of dominant positions, while Article 87 provides for implementing legislation of various kinds and Article 235 for gap-filling legislation where the Treaty lays down an objective without supplying the necessary powers.

Although the Court of Justice often interprets the Treaty in accordance with purposive and teleological principles, the original intent of the authors of the Treaty is frequently unknown, because of the paucity of genuine *travaux préparatoires*, and is of no real importance today. Whatever the authors of the Treaty and the six Member States thought they were doing about mergers in 1957, they left a large gap which the momentum of events in the following decades first highlighted and then began to fill.

I do not propose to take too much time in explaining what happened in the 1960s, 1970s, and the first part of the 1980s. More recent history contains the events and developments which I know best because I was privileged to take part in some of them. At the beginning of 1989 it was far from certain that the Community was going to achieve the goal of securing a Merger Regulation at the end of that year and the events which I shall outline should not be regarded as leading inexorably to that goal. They certainly did not feel like that at the time, nor in retrospect does it seem to me that throughout that year events were bound to lead to a successful conclusion.

By the mid-1960s, it had become apparent to the Commission that competition policy in a common market of six which had settled down and was enjoying considerable success could not stay silent as mergers began to take place in earnest. This was a time of foreign investment and industrial consolidation and no competition policy worthy of the name could ignore what was happening. So, in 1966, the Commission published a Memorandum on Concentration[2] as a result of a study by a group of eminent Professors. Its purpose was to consider whether, and if so how, Articles 85 and 86 together with their implementing Regulation 17 of 1962 could apply to concentrations. But before I go any further, a word about terms of art in Community law.

The Community's legal system has nine official languages and words familiar in law or in everyday language in a Member State frequently have a different and specific meaning in Community law. Examples from competition law are "undertaking" and "concentration". Since what we call loosely the new Merger Regulation is in fact a "Regulation on the control of concentrations between undertakings", the definition of terms is crucial here. One might add that the word "control" in the new Regulation's title also has an unusual meaning, different from the control by one undertaking of another to which the Regulation refers elsewhere. Apart from the humble prepositions, even the title of a Regulation can be mysterious in the European Community! "Undertaking" is a wide term covering almost any independent entity engaged in activities of an economic or commercial nature, from a single inventor or opera singer to a group of companies or a state trading organisation. These are the subjects of our competition rules. "Concentration", in economic terms, means the coming together of resources, assets and power in one set of hands. In Community legal terms, it

[2] "Memorandum on the problem of concentration in the common market", Competition Series, Study No. 3, Brussels, 1966.

covers what we call mergers and acquisitions in English but also other arrangements whereby one undertaking obtains control of another. Article 3 of the new Regulation is entitled "definition of concentration" and attempts to answer what has long been a controversial question in Community law, particularly as regards the dividing line between concentration on the one hand and joint ventures, cooperation agreements and minority shareholdings on the other hand. Control is the key, but what is control and why does the Regulation provide for the *control* of concentrations? Here, the answer is simply that the word is being used in two different senses. In the title, control means to check, to verify, to vet; in the substantive rules of the Regulation, it means to exercise restraint or direction on the free action of another, to dominate, to command. Both senses are to be found in the English dictionary,[3] so for once Community law has not innovated.

The 1966 Memorandum distinguished between concentrations and cartels. The former changed the structure of companies and of the market in which they operated, whereas the latter altered the behaviour of independent undertakings. For several reasons, Article 85 was considered not to be applicable to concentrations. Its very terms, referring to restrictions of competition, possible exemptions and nullity of prohibited agreements, were unsuitable and the procedures and finite exemptions for which Regulation 17 provided were equally inappropriate.[4] However, the Memorandum did

---

[3] E.g. Shorter Oxford English Dictionary, 3rd edition, Vol. I, p. 416.

[4] "To sum up, it may be stated that the distinction generally made in the treatment of cartels and concentrations is necessary and that, for the reasons mentioned, it is not possible to apply Article 85 to agreements whose purpose is the acquisition of total or partial ownership of enterprises or the reorganisation of the ownership of enterprises (merger, acquisition of holdings, purchase of part of the assets). If, after the concentration process, several independent enterprises continue to exist (e.g., in the case of joint ventures), it will be necessary to examine carefully whether, apart from changes in ownership, the participating enterprises did not enter into agreements or concerted practices within the meaning of Article 85, paragraph 1. Furthermore, Article 85, paragraph 1, continues to be applicable if the agreement has as its purpose no permanent change in the ownership but a

conclude that Article *86* was applicable in certain circumstances to concentrations. While the subsequent developments relating to possible application of Article 85 to concentrations are complex and were in the end inconclusive, matters under Article 86 came to a head in 1973 when the European Court of Justice gave judgment in the *Continental Can* case.[5] Article 86, it will be recalled, prohibits an abuse of a dominant position in the common market or a substantial part thereof by one or more undertakings, where trade between Member States may be affected. The Court of Justice held that an abuse may be committed where an undertaking already in a dominant position strengthens or extends that position by acquiring control of another undertaking, thus substantially fettering residual competition in the market concerned. The Court even added to the test that undertakings remaining in the market should be placed in a position of dependence vis-à-vis the dominant undertaking, but this strict proviso was not taken up in later cases on the definition of abuse.

So, in 1973, the newly enlarged Community found itself with an instrument of merger control after all. However, the procedural shortcomings of Regulation 17 and the inadequacies of Article 86 itself became apparent very quickly and the Commission decided to propose to the Council of Ministers the enactment of a Regulation to provide for a dedicated set of rules and procedures for concentrations. It is that proposal, first put forward in 1973 and amended several times since, which was adopted sixteen years later on 21 December 1989.

The basic requirements of a Regulation were self-evident to the Commission: clear substantive rules providing criteria for prohibition and clearance; prior notification, so that we could deal with eggs rather than omelettes; clarification of the relationship between Community rules and national law. Unfortunately, the need for this was not so self-evident to the

---

coordination of the market behaviour of enterprises that remain economically independent."

[5] Case 6/72, *Europemballage and Continental Can Co.* v. *Commission*, [1973] E.C.R. 215.

Member States and the Regulation was nowhere near achieving the requisite unanimity[6] in the Council of Ministers throughout the 1970s and most of the 1980s.

Before considering the acceleration of political interest in the proposal in the late 1980s, let us return briefly to Article 85 which we left on the sidelines as the relationship between Article 86 and merger control got under way.

Article 85 has been applied to joint ventures for a long time. A joint venture brings two undertakings together to carry out a project together. The form and degree of their cooperation and the nature of their project can vary enormously. They may set up a new entity to conduct research and development jointly; they may build a new plant to manufacture a product together; they may combine their distribution networks. The joint venture is a continuum of cooperation arrangements which stretches from very loose consideration of issues of common interest to a merger-like amalgamation of two companies' efforts. Competition lawyers will want to know what the parties were doing before, how long it is to last and what the parties plan to do afterwards.

The real difficulty for present purposes was to draw in a succession of concrete cases a distinction between joint ventures and mergers or concentrations. Theories and doctrines were developed to deal with partial concentrations and asset-swap arrangements. I cannot pretend that the law has always been as clear and readily comprehensible as one would wish. What is important is that Article 85 was brought in a number of cases into close contact with issues most usually connected with concentration and people began to wonder why it could not be applied to concentrations as such. After all, some mergers were agreed between the parties and Article 85 was designed to deal with agreements which restricted competition. Perhaps all three paragraphs of Article 85 could

---

[6] The Regulation was (and is) based on Articles 87 and 235 of the EEC Treaty. Article 235 provides for gap-filling legislation where the Treaty lays down an objective without supplying the necessary powers. It requires unanimity in the Council.

be re-interpreted in the specific context of concentrations so as to provide for a proper approach to merger control. If legislation were needed and Regulation 17 proved inadequate, the Council was empowered by Article 87 to give effect to the principles set out in Articles 85 and 86. Furthermore, provisions under Article 87 required only qualified majority once the first three years of the EEC Treaty's life were over.

The development of Article 85 activity continued, but case law from the Court of Justice on these issues was rare. The first, and indeed the only, major case arose in 1987 and involved various tobacco companies active in the EC market. In 1981, Philip Morris Inc. bought from Rembrandt Group Ltd. one half of Rembrandt's controlling interest in the Rothmans Group. Three other tobacco companies, BAT, R.J. Reynolds and Reemtsma complained to the Commission. The Commission commenced proceedings under Articles 85 and 86. Philip Morris and Rembrandt twice amended their agreements and the Commission eventually decided to close proceedings and to reject the three complaints on the grounds that the amended agreements did not infringe the Treaty rules. BAT and R.J. Reynolds challenged the Commission's decision and the Court of Justice gave judgment on 17 November 1987.[7] The case is interesting on many grounds. For instance, as has already been noted, it is remarkable that with *dramatis personae* from such places as Winston-Salem (North Carolina), New York and Stellenbosch (South Africa),[8] jurisdiction was not put in issue. What is important for present purposes is the question of the application of Article 85 to an agreement whereby an undertaking acquires a shareholding in a competitor. In a judgment that is not without its difficulties of interpretation, the Court held:

> Although the acquisition by one company of an equity interest in a competitor does not in itself constitute conduct restricting competition, such an acquisition may nevertheless serve as an

---

[7] Cases 142 and 156/84, *B.A.T. and R.J. Reynolds* v. *Commission*, [1987] E.C.R. 4487.

[8] See details of parties, E.C.R. at 4566-7.

instrument for influencing the commercial conduct of the companies in question so as to restrict or distort competition on the market in which they carry on business.

That will be true in particular where, by the acquisition of a shareholding or through subsidiary clauses in the agreement, the investing company obtains legal or de facto control of the commercial conduct of the other company or where the agreement provides for commercial cooperation between the companies or creates a structure likely to be used for such cooperation.

That may also be the case where the agreement gives the investing company the possibility of reinforcing its position at a later stage and taking effective control of the other company. Account must be taken not only of the immediate effects of the agreement but also of its potential effects and of the possibility that the agreement may be part of a long-term plan.

Finally, every agreement must be assessed in its economic context and in particular in the light of the situation on the relevant market. Moreover, where the companies concerned are multinational corporations which carry on business on a world-wide scale, their relationships outside the Community cannot be ignored. It is necessary in particular to consider the possibility that the agreement in question may be part of a policy of global cooperation between the companies which are party to it.[9]

The reference to "legal or de facto control" in paragraph 38 of the judgment excited a lot of attention because it seemed to suggest that Article 85 could be applied to concentrations. However, paragraph 31 had said that "since the acquisition of shares in Rothmans International was the subject-matter of agreements entered into by companies which have remained independent after the entry into force of the agreements, the issue must be examined first of all from the point of view of Article 85".[10] There cannot be a concentration if companies remain independent, unless independence is taken in the formal, legal meaning – a meaning usually shunned by competition law in its search for substance and market reality.

Whatever the extent to which the Court's judgment

[9] Paragraphs 37-40, E.C.R. at 4577.
[10] E.C.R. at 4575.

interpreted Article 85 as possibly applying to merger agreements, it certainly emboldened the Commission in its efforts to secure adoption of the Mergers Regulation. My immediate predecessor as competition Commissioner, Peter Sutherland, relaunched the proposed Regulation and set about persuading the Member States, industry and public opinion that its adoption was an urgent necessity. I have nothing but praise for his efforts. When I took office in January 1989, I found the following situation.

The law concerning the application of Articles 85 and 86 to mergers was unclear and industry was worried as a result. The 1992 programme for the completion of the internal market was clearly off the ground and it was widely agreed that a single market needed a single merger policy. Mergers were taking place at an increasing pace and companies were, in any event, coming to the Commission for advice and clearance under Articles 85 and 86 as they assumed that there was a real risk that these provisions might be used to stop mergers which the Commission regarded as unacceptably detrimental to competition. They usually complained that they had to seek approvals from several national authorities as well. It was quite evident that what industry wanted, and legitimately, was to have "one-stop shopping" in merger policy. Mergers which were of a dimension to have a significant effect within the Community should be dealt with by a Community authority whose decision should be final throughout the Community, subject only to judicial review. Articles 85 and 86 could do some of the job, but they were limited and technically inadequate (for example, if there is no agreement or no pre-existing dominant position, they may not apply). Industry did not want to face the agony of a succession of test cases to probe the outer limits of the Treaty. Industry indeed had better things to do in the crucial run up to 1993 than act as guinea-pigs as the European Community felt its way towards merger control. But of course industry was not our only concern. The European citizen and consumer needed protection from damaging industrial concentrations. The European Parliament for its part did not miss an opportunity to urge us to withdraw the Regulation proposal from the Council table and instead get on with applying the Treaty rules audaciously.

As I looked around the Member States and spoke to Ministers, I found very different approaches to merger policy; some tended to see it as a tool of industrial, regional and social policies, a way of shaping industrial structure and location, an opportunity to create European champions to compete overseas with American and Japanese giants. Others saw it as a pure expression of competition principles: monopolisation and market domination should be stopped, everything else should be allowed to proceed. Not all Member States practised at home what they preached in Brussels. Of course not all Member States even had comprehensive merger control systems. Indeed it is fair to say that France, Germany and the UK are alone in having fully developed and regularly applied laws and policies in the merger field.

But I was heartened by three very positive features of the debate. First, there was widespread recognition that there must be Community merger control in the single market. Second, it was increasingly accepted that merger control must be rooted in competition policy. There was much less belief in old-fashioned industrial policy where politicians and bureaucrats sat in their offices playing with industrial structures much as children do with their Lego sets. Third, the Commission's prestige as a responsible and effective enforcer of competition policy was riding high. So the *Zeitgeist* was favourable and the foundations were well laid. But I do not believe that things happen merely because of general political atmosphere, or the movement of historical forces. A lot of hard work, Community-spirited compromise and a statesmanlike approach by Ministers were required to get us our Regulation.

Before turning to the details, I should like to pause a moment longer and consider the historical impact of the Merger Regulation. In what will be seen as the great European year of 1989, the twelve nations of the European Community re-affirmed their commitment to competition as the guiding principle of economic life and their confidence in the European Commission as a policy-making and law enforcement body. The future of the major players in European business who are involved in mergers is now in our hands. The task fills us with pride, but also with humility. If our Community is to play its role in Europe as an anchor of democratic stability and competitive prosperity, competition policy has much to contribute and the adoption of the Merger Regulation is a major and most heartening step towards enhancing that contribution.

The Regulation itself is inevitably easier to understand if one knows the jargon of Community law and practice and the political background. Insiders talk about the Dutch clause and the German clause, the partial concentration clause and the Irish Distillers recital. We must now forget all of that and explain our Regulation from Article 1 to Article 25. At the same time we have to make all the necessary arrangements for entry into force on 21 September 1990. Work is already well under way.

The Regulation applies, as we have seen, to "concentrations". It divides responsibility for the "control of concentrations" between the Commission and the Member States on the basis of turnover thresholds. Our responsibility is for concentrations with a Community dimension, which is defined as meaning those where the aggregate worldwide turnover of all the undertakings concerned is more than five thousand million ECU and the aggregate EC-wide turnover of each of at least two of them is more than 250 million ECU, unless two-thirds of the turnover of each of them occurs in one and the same Member State. The Regulation contains detailed rules for the calculation of turnover, including specially adapted arrangements for banks, insurance companies and other financial institutions. The turnover threshold is a necessarily arbitrary way of defining which concentrations have sufficient impact on the Community as a whole to merit decision by the Commission rather than by Member States. Alternative tests have been considered over the years, but the turnover test is the only one which is both reasonably certain in its application and not excessively complex. Once a concentration meets the Community-dimension criteria, it must be notified to the Commission for analysis. The Commission's first task is to consider whether a properly notified concentration "raises serious doubts as to its compatibility with the common market". This must be done within one month. Compatibility with the common market is determined on the basis of a dominant position analysis. If the concentration creates or strengthens a dominant position as a result of which effective competition would be significantly impeded in the common market or in a substantial part thereof, it is incompatible; if it does not, it is compatible. The Regulation contains a series of factors of which the Commission must take account in making these complex analyses: market structures, competition from inside or outside the Community, the market position of the undertakings concerned and their economic and financial power, the opportunities available to suppliers and users, barriers to entry, supply and demand trends, the consumer interest and the development of technical and economic progress. I have not enumerated all the criteria, but you will have understood that what is called for is detailed market analysis, starting with a precise definition of the relevant product or service market and the geographical market and ending up with a view of the impact of the concentration on competition in those markets. Allow me to focus on three or four of the most controversial issues.

Market definition is always crucial in competition cases and this is nowhere more true than when one is considering the market power of a merged company. Indeed, market power makes no sense whatsoever as a concept unless a market is first defined, both in product or service terms and in geographical terms. Geography here is not political, it is economic. For some products or services, there is a Community market; for others there are still markets covering one or more Member States. There are even world markets for some products or services and in such cases we would take account of the competition brought to the Community by companies situated outside it. But our only concern is for competition *within* the Community and I reject the argument that a competitive world market may justify a dominant position in the Community. Companies will be competitive abroad only if they are used to competing at home. There can be no trade-off between competition in the Community and competitiveness elsewhere. This would be economic nonsense and bad law. Fortunately, the Regulation follows, as it must, the Treaty of Rome in providing for a system of undistorted competition in the common market and I shall resist any attempt to distort competition by distorting the Regulation's meaning.

Another issue which seems to have caused concern is the inclusion of the words borrowed from Article 85(3) of the Treaty "technical and economic progress" in the substantive criteria of the Merger Regulation. It has even been suggested that this opens the back door to industrial policy. This is no more true of the Merger Regulation than it ever has been of Article 85(3). The notion of technical and economic progress must be seen in the context of the competition policy thrust of the Regulation and in conjunction with the specific reference to the consumer interest and the requirement that no obstacle be placed in the way of competition which accompany the notion in the text. This is also reminiscent of Article 85(3) and I expect the Commission to make much the same rounded competition policy analysis of cases before it under the Regulation. The technical and economic progress which a merger may bring about will certainly form part of the Commission's analysis of the reasons for a merger. However, this does not mean that such progress is a legitimate defence for a merger which creates a dominant position. In a competitive market, mergers may or may not give rise to technical and economic progress. In an uncompetitive market, even if they do, they will not be allowed. Indeed, in an uncompetitive market one would not expect to see technical and economic progress in the normal sense of those words at all. There may be some technical progress, but the economic progress would be confined to the dominant company itself in the form of monopoly rents.

Some of the difficulties in understanding these problems of market definition and technical and economic progress seem to arise from a misapprehension of the nature of competition policy analysis. We are not taking a snapshot of a market situation at a particular time. We are looking at the dynamic development of a market and considering the short, medium and long term impact of a given merger. In a time frame in which foreseeable market developments are taken into account, it is perfectly proper to consider wider market issues and the merger's contribution to technical and economic progress. It is in this context too that the reference in a recital to the Community's goal of social and economic cohesion must be understood. Of course, we all seek to encourage economic development in the poorer areas of the Community. Indeed, we believe that competition policy has an important role to play in bringing cohesion about. It would be retrograde and patronising to want to shelter the Community's poorer regions from competition at a time when all over Europe, within and outside the Community's frontiers, people are crying out for the efficiencies and choice which only a market economy can bring alongside democratic political structures. Competition will lead to cohesion and the dynamics of the Community's integration process require that merger policy be part of that general movement. Once again, this means that there is no cohesion defence to dominant positions. But it does mean that market integration as part of the cohesion process is a factor of which account is properly taken in analysing a given merger case.

On the substantive criteria in the Regulation, the question is bound to be asked whether it is sufficient to know what Article 86 means to understand the dominant position test or whether the qualification "as a result of which effective competition would be significantly impeded" gives rise to a new test altogether. In my view, we are at the beginning of a new legal development and the Council did not wish to create a pure dominant position test. A dominant position as such is not prohibited. You may ask whether a dominant position without the effect of impeding competition is at all conceivable. I think that in most cases it is not. However, the dynamic factor of time is again important here. A short-lived market share of some size in a market with no or low barriers to entry is not really a threat to competition at all. The Court of Justice has traditionally defined dominance in Article 86 cases in terms of independence or the ability to act with scant regard to competitive pressures. This is not quite the same as impeding competition and I expect a new line of case law to develop. The starting point for any analysis will of course remain Article 86 and the court's case law on that provision, until new case law is developed under the Regulation. It seems to me, therefore, that an understanding of Article 86 is what is needed to commence analysis of a merger under the Regulation. In addition, one must begin to develop analysis of the significant impediment to competition which the merger may create. This analysis will require consideration of the way in which supply, price and output decisions are likely to be constrained and will not be very different from the traditional analysis under Article 86. I am reluctant in this regard to attempt to quantify these issues. Our American friends have tried to apply concentration indices and to consider reactions to hypothetical price increases at certain levels, but I am not persuaded that this has always been successful. As it is on all these issues, my mind is open on the question of possible Commission guidelines and we will be considering the requirements of European industry as well as the American experience before making any commitments in this respect.

I do not propose to say very much about the definition of concentration and the relationship between that concept and joint ventures. This is not because I underestimate the importance of this issue or the difficulties to which it has given rise in the past. The Commission intends to issue guidelines on this very point and drafts are already circulating for comment. The one point I wish to stress now is that our approach is an economic, rather than legal one. Competition law is rightly concerned with substance rather than form. The Regulation itself attempts to define the notion of concentration as clearly as possible. The guidelines will provide further assistance and we look forward to receiving your comments on the drafts which you may already have seen. The key issue, which has to be fleshed out in detail, is whether a transaction brings about a lasting change in market structure or merely a temporary change in companies' behaviour. The former is a concentration, the latter is not.

Immediate analysis must be made within one month of notification. If we have no serious doubts, a decision will be issued saying so and that, subject only to two possible exceptions, is the end of the matter. The concentration may proceed without any fear of disturbance by national or Community competition authorities. This is likely to be the case with a large majority of proposed mergers and for them the change brought about by this procedure will be a considerable one. They will benefit from a one-stop shop, where there is one analysis by one authority on the basis of competition criteria which takes one month and is binding throughout the European Community.

If there are serious doubts about a concentration's compatibility with the common market, a further analysis becomes necessary. Formal proceedings are opened and must be completed within four months. The results of these proceedings will be prohibition or approval of the concentration, with or without conditions, by means of a finding of incompatibility or compatibility. And, once again, subject to only two exceptions, the Commission's decision is final throughout the Community and is reviewable only by the Community's Courts.

Our purpose in applying these rules when they enter into force on 21 September will be to keep markets competitive by preventing their being dominated in a way which impedes the maintenance or development of effective competition. This means that our attention will normally be attracted by horizontal mergers between companies in the same market, but there could also be vertical or conglomerate cases where a concentration of economic and financial power proves to be inimical to competition. The application of the Regulation's criteria to particular market situations, industries and circumstances will be made clear in case law and, if need be, in Commission guidelines.

The thresholds are the key to the division of responsibilities between the Commission and the Member States. The Commission and several Member States believe that the threshold levels are too high. It is neither in the Community's interest nor in that of its companies for many mergers with an impact on the Community-wide market still to be subject to a multitude of national controls. We are confident that, within four years, the Council will be persuaded that the thresholds must come down. The Regulation provides that the Commission will make a proposal on which the Council will decide by qualified majority. Some commentators have wondered whether a provision in a Regulation adopted by unanimity can be properly amended by qualified majority. For myself, I see no reason why it should not and this was a view taken unanimously by the Council with the backing of the Commission. I would remind you that the Regulation is based not only on Article 235, which requires unanimity, but also on Article 87 which requires qualified majority.

Articles 85 and 86 go some way in applying competition policy to mergers, or concentrations to use the Community term of art, and therefore Article 87 is the proper legal basis for the implementation of the principles set out in Articles 85 and 86 to mergers. However, Article 235 is necessary to deal with those parts of the merger phenomenon which Articles 85 and 86 do not reach. Since Article 87 provides explicitly for Council legislation by qualified majority "to determine the relationship between national laws and the provisions contained in this section or adopted pursuant to this Article", I am confident that the Treaty envisages qualified majority for legislation amending the thresholds dividing the Commission's merger jurisdiction from that of the Member States. I expect to make proposals to the Council to bring the thresholds level down during the lifetime of this Commission.

As I have said, above the thresholds the Commission has exclusive jurisdiction. The Member States may invoke two exceptions to our exclusive jurisdiction, and there is one exception to their exclusive jurisdiction. Let me say at once that all these exceptions are narrowly circumscribed and I do not expect them to be used frequently. The first is contained in Article 9, soberly entitled "referral to the competent authorities of the Member States". This provision was included at the request of Germany and proved controversial with other Member States. But the very special, almost Constitutional, position of competition policy in Germany, and that country's consequent reluctance to cede total control to the Commission even above the thresholds, made some sort of concession essential if agreement was to be reached. We would not, however, have accepted wording which enabled Member States to claw back cases which we had already decided and where we saw no real basis for separate national consideration of the matter. What was ultimately agreed was that a Member State may inform the Commission that it considers that a concentration threatens to create or strengthen a dominant position in a distinct market within its territory. This notification must take place within three weeks of the Member State's receipt from the Commission of a copy of the notification. The Commission then considers the Member State's application and may either decide that the case merits examination on this basis by the Commission itself, or refer it to the national authorities of the country concerned so that national competition law may be applied, or decide that the Member State's application is unfounded because there is no relevant "distinct" market or no threat of a dominant position. Time limits and guidance on relevant market definition are provided and the Commission remains master of the procedure. This is one of two exceptions to the principle that the Commission has exclusive jurisdiction in respect of cases above the thresholds. This provision was politically necessary, but it is narrowly circumscribed and likely to be applied very infrequently.

The other gateway to national jurisdiction relates to what are described as "other legitimate interests". All Member States and the Community institutions share a fundamental commitment to the pursuit of competition policy. However, there are other legitimate interests which may arise in merger cases and which are not, or at least not yet or not fully, subject to Community rules. Where a Member State has a legitimate non-competition interest to protect, it may take appropriate measures which comply with Community law. Three examples of legitimate interests are given: public security, media plurality and prudential rules. If, as a result of a merger above the Regulation's thresholds, a Member State finds itself with an arms manufacturer in the hands of a group which also supplies to unfriendly foreign Governments, or with one person or company owning too many publications, radio stations or television channels, or with a person or company who is unfit and improper owning a financial institution, then, notwithstanding the Commission's verdict on the competition aspects of the merger, the Member State may take any appropriate measures to remedy the situation. Those measures must, in accordance with the general principle of proportionality in Community law, be the minimum necessary to achieve the goal being pursued as a legitimate interest and must not breach any other rule or principle of Community law. The three examples given are not exhaustive because it is impossible to foresee all possible national legitimate interests. A procedure is therefore provided for Member States to apply to the Commission for recognition of other non-competition legitimate interests. The Member State may not take any measures before the Commission has decided whether the interest claimed is compatible with Community law. The Commission must take its decision within one month of the Member State's application.

These two exceptions should not detract from the Regulation's basic principle set out in Article 21(2): "No Member State shall apply its national legislation on competition to any concentration that has a Community-dimension". That deals with cases above the thresholds. Below them, the Member State's jurisdiction is in principle exclusive and the Commission will not interfere. Here too there is one exception, inserted at the request of Italy, the Netherlands and Belgium. Article 22(3) provides that if the Commission finds at the request of a Member State that a concentration *without* Community-dimension creates or strengthens a dominant position as a result of which effective competition would be significantly impeded within that Member State's territory, the Commission may, if the concentration affects trade between Member States, take the decisions provided for in the Regulation to safeguard competition. This provision was necessary because some Member States have no effective merger control system either because their economies are so open that most competition problems have a large element of extraterritoriality or for other political reasons. In any case, the Commission may intervene only at the request of a Member State, and not of its own motion. Furthermore, our involvement will be limited to ensuring that competition is safeguarded; a Member State can ask us to oppose a merger which endangers competition in its territory, not to allow one which it favours to proceed. This provision is therefore narrowly defined and would not permit the Commission to deal with mergers below the threshold on a general basis, even if it were inclined to evade the spirit of the threshold provision in this way. It is consequently one which is also likely to be infrequently applied.

One issue which must not be forgotten in this division of responsibilities between Community and national law is the nature of the Community rules themselves. Articles 85 and 86 apply to certain concentrations and no Regulation can abrogate the Treaty and the interpretation placed upon it by the European Court of Justice. But the Commission has told the Member States that it does not intend to enforce the Treaty provisions under the threshold levels at which it believes that concentrations will not normally affect trade between Member States significantly: 2000 MECU and 100 MECU respectively for the two main thresholds. In addition, the Regulation repeals the implementing Regulations for Articles 85 and 86 in respect of concentrations. The effect of this is that the Commission is denied the panoply of powers and procedures needed to apply the Treaty rules effectively, while the national courts may not apply Article 85. They may, however, apply Article 86, which does not require any implementing legislation to be directly effective, while the

Commission still has residual enforcement powers under Article 89 of the Treaty. There is no way of completely ruling out litigation probing the Commission's policy, which is of course designed to reinforce the central concept of the one-stop shop. But the Regulation states clearly in Article 22(1) that it "alone shall apply to concentrations as defined in Article 3". The fundamental policy objective is clear: to set up a simple, predictable and clear Community merger control system with the Commission responsible for cases above the thresholds and the Member States below. The technicalities of Community law and the requirements of Community politics explain the interplay between fundamental principle and circumscribed derogation which characterizes the Regulation, rather as it does the EEC Treaty itself. I cannot, any more than any other honest politician, offer legislative perfection. What I can offer is the Commission's commitment to implement the Regulation fully and fairly in the light of its stated policy objectives: competition in the single market; merger analysis based on examination of markets as they really operate; and clear demarcation between the competence of the Commission and that of the Member States.

The signal from Europe to the rest of the world is clear: the Community re-affirms its faith in competition and in the Commission as a policy-making and law enforcement body. I should point out that the Community's rules on jurisdiction in competition cases apply to mergers as well. Any concentration, wherever conceived or born, involving any undertakings, wherever located, must be notified if it meets the threshold requirements. If the significant amount of business within the Community required by the thresholds occurs, the merger will engage our jurisdiction. Any remedies ordered by the Commission as a result of proceedings under the Regulation will of course take account of the interests of foreign States in accordance with the comity principle. Nevertheless, to use the jurisdictional language of our Court of Justice, there can be no doubt that mergers which are liable to have a significant impact on the competitive structure of our market are *implemented* in our territory. Our jurisdiction will be engaged and we shall exercise it to safeguard competition in the Community market.

In this context there may be conflicts of jurisdiction, for example with the United States. If the case is a sufficiently important one the consequence could be an unseemly and damaging dispute. At present there is no means of resolving such a dispute. I therefore think that we now need to give serious consideration to the drawing up of a Treaty or less formal agreement between the Community and the United States to deal with such problems.

Such an agreement would provide for information gathering and exchange and would lay down a detailed procedure for consultations on cases and issues of common interest. It might even contain an arbitration clause, although the political difficulties of getting that agreed should not be underestimated. But even without one I would welcome such a development as I believe that we have much to gain from working together in this field. I will want to consider carefully the response to this idea, and if it is sufficiently positive I certainly intend to pursue it further.

The other international issue in the Regulation which has given rise to comment is dealt with in Article 24, entitled "Relations with non-member countries". This is most emphatically not a reciprocity clause. The handling of individual cases will not be affected by any consideration of whether the merger in question would have been permitted in the country of origin of any of the companies involved. Member States are merely entitled to inform the Commission of general difficulties encountered by their undertakings in respect of concentrations in a non-member country. The Commission will report to the Council and make appropriate recommendations. If it appears that a non-member country does not afford Community undertakings treatment comparable to that which the Community affords its undertakings, the Commission may ask the Council for a negotiating mandate with a view to obtaining such comparable treatment for Community undertakings.

It should not be thought that the Regulation will be

administered by the Commission in isolation. In addition to the close involvement of the Member States' authorities in an Advisory Committee, the Regulation makes detailed provision for "due process rights" for the actual parties to the proceedings, the undertakings. They have the right to reply to any allegations we make and to be heard before we take a decision. Third parties may also take part in the proceedings by responding to our invitation to comment which will be made in every case by means of a publication in the Official Journal of the European Communities.

The Commission is the body set up by the Treaty of Rome to administer competition policy and is now making all the necessary preparations to implement the merger Regulation. The policy decisions to be made under the Regulation are quite properly a matter for the Commission, subject as it is to judicial review by the Court of Justice and political scrutiny by the European Parliament. I am therefore opposed to the notion that a special European competition agency should be set up outside the Commission. A Treaty revision would in any case be necessary for that. But the main objection is that it would be wholly unacceptable for the controversial policy decisions which will inevitably have to be made to be handed over to a body which would not be accountable at all, and only add to controversy if the agency were able to make decisions which the Commission was then entitled to overrule.

In conclusion, therefore, this Regulation which is an important Community development from the political, economic and legal points of view also confirms the Community's seriousness as a major player in the world's political, economic and legal systems. I have not sought to provide you with a comprehensive commentary on the Regulation. Moreover, the development of merger control in EEC competition law, the title of this lecture, is only just beginning. I have added a second chapter setting out the principles which will guide the interpretation and application of the new Regulation. But, as implementation gets under way, let us pause and consider the Regulation's political significance. Twelve old nations of Western Europe have formed a Community, soon to fulfil its original promise of full market integration. Those nations, with their different levels of economic and industrial development, their different political outlooks, indeed their different comprehension and apprehension of competition policy, have given the European Community a strong, independent, market-driven system of merger control. The Commission has the fact-finding and enforcement powers which it needs. More importantly, the Community has the merger policy which *it* needs as we move into the single market with all the restructuring of industry which that entails. Finally, the range of competition policy has been completed, thus reinforcing the Community's ability to fulfil what many now see to be its historical task in this generation: to provide the democratic, peaceful, prosperous magnet and anchor in the transition from the cold war to the new Europe. I started this lecture with a reference to the role of the Community in post-war reconciliation in Western Europe. That role, so successfully played in the Franco-German theatre, now has to be repeated on the wider European stage. It is no longer so much a question of reconciling old enemies, although that may still be necessary; we have to provide an example for fragile democracies and even more vulnerable economies.

Our neighbours in central and eastern Europe look at the Community and they admire the industrial achievements of all its countries. Looking more closely, for example, they also see Spain which has emerged from dictatorship and corporatist economics to become a dynamic democracy and market-based economy. Then they see what binds the twelve Member States together in a Community and notice that at the heart of its successful market economy lies a sound competition policy. Competitive structures must be safeguarded and that is the role of merger policy. The Community today has the instrument and the policy to fulfil the promise of undistorted competition made in 1957 by the authors of the Treaty of Rome in Article 3(f). We have waited a long time for this, but it is perhaps fitting that the Regulation should have been adopted in 1989. For that was the year in which the dismantling of barriers which is at the heart of the

Community's internal market programme became the watch-word for the rest of Europe, taking on a new and deeper political meaning as it spread.

B. SOME ISSUES OF INTERPRETATION AND ADMINISTRATION

Merger Control is a complex matter of legal and economic analysis. Any new regulation is bound to raise questions of interpretation. But in relation to its subject matter, it cannot be said that the Regulation is excessively complicated. It provides for a competition-based framework in which the analysis of all mergers meeting its jurisdictional requirements will be assessed. While it not possible, or even desirable, to lay down a scientific test to be applied in a mechanical way to any case which may come up, the Regulation can leave no one in doubt about its true purpose and content.

The Commission's concern will be to determine whether a merger threatens competition by creating or strengthening a dominant position. The Regulation contains a number of factors which will have to be considered in making that determination. The impact of a merger on the properly defined market will be the fundamental issue. We will have to look at market trends over the range of products and services involved.

The Regulation includes "technical and economic progress" as one of the matters to be considered. There has been widespread misunderstanding about this phrase. It is taken from the Treaty of Rome itself and has been applied with no great difficulty for 30 years as part of the Community's competition law. It is, in general competition law and under the Regulation, an important element of the essentially wider analysis which includes the impact of a transaction on the consumer interest and on competition in the market or markets concerned.

Lest there be any doubt, let me stress that no words plucked from the Regulation can give rise to a defence against the finding that there is a dominant position as a result of which competition is significantly impeded. If that is the finding, then the merger may not proceed. If, on the other hand, no dominant position is found to exist as a result of which competition is impeded, then the merger may proceed without further ado. The Regulation amounts to no more than that. It could hardly be otherwise, because I do not see how a dominant position which impedes competition could give rise to technical or economic progress of the sort which competition policy could endorse. There may be some short-term technical progress available to a monopolist, but it would not last for long when one considers the well known debilitating effect of monopoly. As for economic progress, apart from monopoly rents which would accrue, there would be no progress at all. Competition policy is directed at consumer welfare and the enhancement of competitiveness which the drive to satisfy consumer welfare engenders. It is through that route that the interests of consumer and industry alike are served and economic progress furthered.

To bring that about we have set up the teams and systems needed to make the Regulation work. A Task Force has been established within DG IV and we have recruited to it some of the very best officials from within the Commission and on secondment from the competition authorities of the Member States. I am delighted with the cooperative spirit in which this has been done. We have set up the most modern and sophisticated computer systems and security arrangements in order to provide for the rapid and secure treatment of information received. The preparatory measures we have taken have all been very well received and they augur well for the efficiency of the operation on which we are now embarking.

The heart of the Regulation's system is of course the division of labour between the Commission and the Member States. This is the *one stop shop* which European industry needed so much and which several of the Member States regarded as one of the main attractions of the Regulation. Are they getting it after all?

Jurisdiction to deal with cases under the regulation is divided by means of a threshold. We chose a purely arithmetical threshold based on turnover, above which the Commission normally has exclusive jurisdiction and below which the Member States normally have exclusive jurisdiction. Over the years other possible criteria had been examined. But the Member States ultimately unanimously agreed on the turnover criterion precisely because they regarded a clear-cut determinant of jurisdiction as of prime importance. Let us look at how this will work in practice. A merger or acquisition, meeting the definition of concentration to use the catch-all Community term, will be notified to the Commission if it exceeds the turnover threshold. The case will then be for the Commission to consider under the regulation's rules and procedures. There will be no Member State jurisdiction to consider such a merger. There are only two narrowly circumscribed exceptions to the Commission's exclusive jurisdiction over cases above the threshold.

Under Article 9 of the Regulation, a Member State may make an application to the Commission, saying that a particular merger threatens to create or strengthen a dominant position within its territory or part of its territory. It should be noted that the Member State cannot say that it rather likes a particular merger but only that it is worried that it might have anti-competitive effects within its territory. So, the Member State writes to the Commission saying that a merger is dangerous. What can the Commission do?

It can agree with the Member State that the merger is a particular threat to competition within that Member State's territory and refer the case to the competition authorities of that Member State for analysis under the normal procedures applicable in that State. This possibility has led to the view that this is a loophole in the regulation. In fact it is no such thing, because the Commission may take two other, quite different decisions on the application by the Member State.

It may, still agreeing with the Member State that there is a threat to competition in the territory concerned, decide to take the case up itself by applying the normal rules and procedures of the Regulation. In this case, there is no referral to the national authorities.

Finally, the Commission may *disagree* with the Member State's application and find that there is no threat to competition. This could be, for example, because the Commission rejects the Member State's argument that its territory is a relevant market in competition policy terms. In such cases the Commission would simply inform the Member State of its decision that the application should be rejected. There would be no referral back and that would be the end of the matter, subject only to judicial review by the European Court.

I think that all fair-minded observers will agree that there is no breach here of the one stop shopping principle. The Commission is firmly in the driving seat in deciding whether or not a case is better dealt with at Community or national level, if there is indeed a case at all. I see this as a sensible extension of the division of labour at the heart of the Regulation.

The second, and the only other exception to the principle of exclusive jurisdiction above the threshold is contained in Article 21 of the Regulation. This concerns the public or legitimate interest which a Member State may wish to seek to pursue on non-competition grounds. Once again, this is not a general public interest exception to the Regulation's rule of jurisdiction. I am grateful for the opportunity to dispel this misunderstanding. The Regulation, as I have said, is rooted in competition policy and its only purpose is to apply that policy in a systematic and comprehensive way. It does not pretend to solve other problems which may arise as a result of a merger. Mergers have direct consequences on markets. They may also have indirect consequences, or side-effects, for other areas of public policy. In discussion with the Member States, we were able to identify three such areas: public security, plurality of the media and prudential rules for the financial service industries. A merger may be perfectly innocent in competition terms, but have undesirable consequences in any of these three fields for a Member State. In these circumstances, it is perfectly reasonable for the Member State to be able to take the measures necessary to give effect to its policy in this regard notwithstanding the decision reached by the Commission on the merger on competition grounds. This is once again a sensible division of work between the Commission and the Member States which takes account of the realities of Community politics and law.

The three areas I have mentioned are identified specifically in the Regulation. A Member State will therefore be able to take the necessary measures, but only the necessary measures, in order to provide for public security, media plurality and respect for prudential rules in the context of a merger under the Commission's jurisdiction. The measures taken by the Member State must be the minimum necessary to achieve the objective in question and must always be in full compliance with the general principles and rules of Community law. The Commission will be vigilant in applying this provision.

The three areas of public interest identified in the Regulation may not be exhaustive. The Regulation takes account of this by providing for an application procedure, whereby a Member State communicates to the Commission any other claim of public interest. The Commission will then have to consider the Member State's application in the light of the general principles and provisions of Community law and give the Member State an answer within one month. The Member State may not take any measures until the Commission has given its decision. Once again, I think it is perfectly clear that this is not a general loophole or exception to the one stop shop principle. It most certainly does *not* enable a Member State to claim the right to stop any merger it disapproves of by claiming that it has a legitimate interest to object to the merger. The Commission remains in charge of the authorisation procedures and will accept intervention by the Member States only where it is compatible with the Regulation's underlying principles and Community law more generally.

It should not be thought that the one stop shop principle was designed to please the Commission and industry alone. The Member States, all of them, as I have said, were fully committed to this idea. The Regulation would not have been adopted without it. Indeed, it is right to say that the enthusiasm of some Member States which had been recalcitrant during earlier stages of negotiation was brought about largely by the focusing of attention on the one stop shop as one of the principal merits of the Regulation.

I therefore expect Member States to avail themselves of these two limited exceptions sparingly. We will keep our side of the bargain, by applying this Regulation as an instrument of competition policy at the service of the Community's internal market, and by not seeking to use it for other purposes.

We will also respect fully the basic principle of exclusive jurisdiction for the Member States *below* the threshold. There is one exception to that exclusive jurisdiction, the third and final exception to the general principle. Once again, I shall show that it is circumscribed and should not give rise to many difficulties in practice. Article 22(3) provides that the Commission may intervene under the Regulation in respect of mergers which create or strengthen a dominant position as a result of which competition is impeded within the territory of a Member State, even if the thresholds for Community competence are not met. This may look like a general exception to the one stop shop principle. But it is not, and the Regulation would not have been adopted if any such provision had been included. The Commission may intervene under this exception *only* if a Member State asks it to do so in respect of a competition problem in *its* territory. In other words, this is a sort of agency arrangement whereby a Member State may call upon the Commission to deal with a competition problem within its territory. There is no question of double jeopardy or multiple shopping. It is a simple extension of the cooperation which prevails in the competition field between the Commission and the Member States.

I have said that these three exceptions are the only ones to one stop shopping. Some commentators have tried to complicate things further by suggesting that the Commission will still apply Articles 85 and 86 of the Rome Treaty to mergers and acquisitions falling under the Regulation's thresholds. Let me say at once that I have no intention of seeking the application of those provisions. This Regulation is an effective and comprehensive implementation of the Community's competition principles to mergers and acquisitions.

I should say that the thresholds contained in the Merger Regulation are too high for our liking and that we expect to see them come down within four years. Nevertheless, we will loyally apply the Regulation as it stands and will not anticipate the lower thresholds which I confidently expect the Council to adopt in due course by qualified majority.

In all our endeavours under the Regulation, we will enjoy the close and constant cooperation with the Member States which has been such a hallmark of competition policy in the Community since the 1960s. It is quite wrong to portray the national competition authorities as the rivals or adversaries of the Commission. We are all on the same side, doing similar things with the same objectives. The history of Community competition policy shows that cooperation, not conflict, has been the order of the day between the national and Community competition bodies. The Merger Regulation will also benefit from this cooperation. The national competition authorities will receive copies of important documents and will come together as an Advisory Committee to express their view to the Commission. But of course it will be the Commission alone that takes the decisions. The clear division of tasks brought about by the Regulation will mean that there will be no scope for argument about jurisdiction between the Commission and Member States. The turnover threshold was chosen as a criterion for that very purpose. It is in some ways a blunt and even arbitrary instrument, but it has the great merit of clarity.

Let me sum up, therefore, on this crucial point of relations between Community jurisdiction and national jurisdiction by saying that I know I can expect the full cooperation of the Member States in applying our procedures and in showing respect for the division of jurisdiction brought about by the Regulation in determining who handles a particular case. The unequivocal acceptance of the basic principle of one stop shopping is as much in their interest as ours, and I know they too will want that to be clear. The three exceptions which I have explained are narrowly circumscribed and will be applied restrictively. Each application will have to be justified carefully and I will need a lot of persuading before an exception can be relied upon in either direction.

I have dealt extensively with the jurisdiction of the Commission and the Member States, because that issue lies at the heart of the Regulation. I am well aware that, in our increasingly inter-dependent world, there are other, third country jurisdictions which may also be interested in cases before us. This is not a new problem, since both we in the Commission and the Member States are well aware of the problems of conflicts of jurisdiction in competition matters. I have proposed to look carefully at this issue with the United States of America and we may in due course be able to make a big step forward in international relations in this regard. An agreement between the European Community and the US, in whatever form, could serve as a model for dealing with competition questions in international trade.

The substantive analysis of mergers under the Regulation will be very much a matter of market analysis and definition. I will want to know from my advisers what the product or service market is in a given case and what is the geographical market in which the companies concerned compete. The market integration process in the Community is accelerating as we approach 1993 and detailed analysis of competitive forces will be necessary in every case before a reliable market definition can be made. Once that is done, I will need to assess the impact of the merger on the market. The question whether or not a dominant position results from a merger will entail a precise assessment of the capabilities of competitors in the market and the prospects of market entry by others. The debate about barriers to entry and market contestability will therefore be at the centre of our examination of the cases. I am not sure that the time has come, however, if indeed it ever will, to lay down arithmetical indices for the measurement of market power. But all the tools of economic analysis will be used in drawing up a complete picture. I will want to check economic analysis against what has been happening in the market. If barriers to entry are claimed not to exist, I will want to look at the actual facts of market entry attempts and the historical development of market shares.

Beyond market share itself as a factor, I will look at the extent to which the merged company has a hold over important resources, supply or distribution channels. The starting point of this analysis will be similar to that already carried out under Article 86 of the Treaty of Rome. That should not be surprising, because the dominant position test is to be found there as well. However, just as under Article 86 the analysis goes on to consider the *abuse* of the dominant position, here too dominant position is not the end of the matter and we have to consider the impediment to competition which the dominant position may create. It is hard to conceive of a dominant position which does not impede competition, because a market in which dominance is possible is likely to have high barriers to entry and the attainment or strengthening of dominance is likely to raise those barriers even higher. The addition of the impediment to competition test reminds us that market dominance is a dynamic concept which must be considered over a certain period of time. It is the impact of the dominant position on competition and on the ability of companies to contest or enter a particular market which concerns us. Relatively higher market shares, together with other factors which suggest dominance, may not in themselves necessarily be decisive considerations if the market under examination is genuinely open to competition. Nonetheless, I accept the general prejudice of competition policy that higher market shares, sustained over a period of time, suggest that a market is not contestable, even if this is not to be regarded as an irrebuttable presumption.

Our purpose in all this will be to maintain undistorted competition as the fundamental driving force of our economy. Markets which remain competitive are those which will satisfy consumers and enhance the competitiveness of industry. They need no interference from us at the Commission. Only those mergers which threaten competition by allowing companies to dominate markets will be stopped.

I am sometimes asked if we will look at competition in world markets as well. There is an important distinction to be made here. The only market with which we are allowed to be concerned when assessing the impact of a merger is the European Community, or some substantial part of it. However, there are many sectors in which competition within the Community genuinely extends beyond the Community's borders. In such cases, it is perfectly proper to look at the competition brought to the Community from outside. If companies in third countries are competing or are capable of competing within the Community, their market share or other manifestation of competitive pressure should of course be considered in any assessment of competition in the Community market. In such cases, I will have no hesitation in including foreign companies in the analysis of a merger before me.

In conclusion, we will of course have many difficult problems of economic and legal analysis before us. I am confident that we have the people and the systems to do the job properly. I have set out very clear objectives to the Merger Task Force in DG IV: rapid, fair procedures and competitive markets. The Commission has been given considerable responsibilities under this Regulation. The structure of the Community economy and the livelihoods of thousands of people will be at stake. I count on the cooperation of the Member States, industry and its advisors in helping us to administer the Regulation properly.

INDEX